33 Degrees Angle. Designing Trajectory Death By Default.

President JF. Kennedy's Afterlife before the Council of Creation, .Ya, .devil & The Council of .Ra

David Gomadza

PAPERBACK ISBN: 9798323906505:

DEDICATION

A better future.

CONTENTS

ACKNOWLEDGMENTS

Tomorrow's World Order

33 DEGREES ANGLE. DESIGNING TRAJECTORY DEATH BY DEFAULT.

The Council of Ra .Ra Designing Trajectory Death by Default
Now if the sun gives you hope love and life then the sun can also remove these by default assume when you die you go to hell then by default hell is the sole purpose of life but what if this is not the case then we can say that death is not the end but means to an end what if we Ask what can be done then the answer is that a lot can be done but how if we are to argue about life and death then life come first then death but what when there is no life first but death how can we manicure this paradigm?
If we are to ask what could be then this is the answer we might be in such a state of mistrust and disbelief but if we Ask what could be then you will see that if we Ask what can be after what could be then you can see that a lot of answers comes up to us that means the possibilities changes only after asking what could be
Now what are these options if I Ask
1 the ability not to die comes up as an option
2 ability to cheat death
3 ability to evade justice
4 the ability to ask why and when
5 what can be and how
6 what would be
7 what if but
8 what is but when
9 what was but how
10 what if [asked after all these questions]
11 what is to be
12 what would be
13 what is to be

14 what could be
15 what us to be
16 what would be
17 what is to be
18 what could be
19 what was to be
20 what could be
21 what is to be
22 what would be
23 what is to be
24 what would be
25 what was be
26 what is to be
27 what can be
28 what is to be
29 what and when
30 what is to be
31 what was but could be
32 what could be but what if
33 what was but is not
34 what could be but is not
35 what is to be but how
36 what was To be but would not be
37 what can be but how and when
38 what is and how come
39 what is but cant be
40 what would be but when
41 what can be but how and not when
42 what would be but if and when
43 what is to be but
44 what would be but if when
45 what is to be but how come
46 what can be but what if
47 what would be but when
48 what was but might not be
49 what is but is not to be
50 what can't be but how
Now that we have looked at the most critic questions that must be answered then we must ask what can be but
Now if we Ask what was but is not then we get a new set of questions altogether this alone points to another possibility of what could be

Now if we Ask another way then we can even get another set of different questions altogether does all this point to a different possibility of life after death? To answer this we must ask critical questions that can give us concrete solutions

Now what is the purpose of life is life there so that at the end of time we go to heaven or life to some like the god .Ra there to be manipulated and used to deprive others of their rights to go to .Ya [God]

Now let's look at the famous case study of the president of the United States JF. Kennedy from now on abbreviated as JFK

if we Ask a lot of questions then these are the questions

1 what can be
2 what could be
3 what was
4 what is to be
5 what would be
6 what was but is not
7 what could be but
8 what is to be but
9 what is to be but
10 what is but is not
11 what can be but
12 what would be but is not
13 what can be but is not
14 what would be but when
15 what is to be but
16 what can be but
17 what is to be but
18 what was but when
19 what is but cant be
20 what was but might not be
21 what is to be but how come
22 what can be but if when
23 what is and why
24 what can be but when
25 what is to be
26 what can be
27 what is to be but
28 what was but
29 what would be but when
30 what is to be but ask when

31 what is but is not
32 what has been but is not
33 what I'd but can't be
34 what would be but when
35 what is but after what
36 what I'd but when
37 what would be but what if
38 what must be but when
39 what is but when
40 what is but what if
41 what can be but how
42 what is but when
43 what would be but after what
44 what is to be
45 what would be46 what when is to be
46 what if
47 what if and when
48 what if and how
49 what can be and how
50 what is but what then
51 what is but why
52 what is but how come
53 what to be but what if
54 when and how
55 what if but with reservations
56 what is but when
57 what can be but what if
58 what was but can still be
59 when and why
60 what is but when
61 what would be but with what
62 what is
63 what is but what if
64 when and why
65 what is to be but
66 what can be but how come
67 what will be
68 what will be but when and how
69 what if but
70 what might be but when
71 what is but

72 what was but can't be
73 what is but can still be
74 what might be but when
75 what would be
76 what is
77 what is not
78 when and how
79 what to do
80 what can be done
81 what if
82 what was but can't be
83 what can be be but
84 what is but when
85 what would be
86 what might be
87 what is to be but when
88 when and how
89 what is and who is
90 to be is to be but when
91 what can be but how
92 what would be and when
93 what can be
94 what is but cant be
95 what has been but how come
96 what if we can
97 what was to be
98 what would be
99 what can be
100 what could be

If we look at all these questions one by one at the end you can see a pattern developing one that says life is not just to go to .Ya life can go somewhere else but where is the question if we care to ask our selves what can be then this is the answer life can be frustrated in such a way that life might not be to go to .Ya what if life is about ascending Yahweh?

But more sinister what if there is someone out there who calculates and do magic thinking to frustrate the main reason of creation to stop people going to heaven and present their case before Yahweh ladies and gentlemen what I am about to reveal is something out of this world you will never hear this from somewhere else because these are the closely guarded secrets of he gods especially .Ra god if we look at how and why then we can see a pattern developing .Ra is more than just a God but the cleverest of all deities for him alone has the power to manipulate things and defeat the purpose of creation

Now let's look at a famous case study that of the president of the United States JFK in detail

Introduction

JFK was assassinated by according to reports a one Oswald Lee Harvey but what I am going to reveal has never been revealed before the reason being that this is a closely guarded secret but nevertheless something we must reveal the president was shoot at an angle which we now know as 33,9998672 degrees as a Trajectory from the Texas School Book Depository

Now we can also look at this Trajectory as a reference to the gods for it is a common number to them we know this because this number is common to most special events 1 death of Jesus at age 33

2 life of Yahweh at 33

3 drowning of Hercules at 33

4 death of Plato at 33

5 death of Cesar 33

6 death of Heroborah the greek god

7 death of Atopheres

8 death of Horondus

9 death of Anthena

10 resurrection of Jesus

11 resurrection of Plato

12 resurrection of Horoundas

13 ascension of Ceasar and his death few months after

14 ascension of Queen Sheba at 33

15 ascension of King Madras at 33

Now if we ask what is the most common thing between then this is the answer they are all 33 years old and what is the significance of this numbér if we look at this number then we cañ see that it is not just any number because it's frequency is 38 which is the normal daily temperature for a typical day but more important it is a value associated with .Ra the god of the sun if we Ask. Ra the significance of 33 then this is the answer 33 signifies the angle at which humans can Trajectory around the sun without emitting any brain thoughts it is only at this angle that a person cannot emit brain thoughts to the atmosphere that means anyone whose thoughts are at this angle will never be known what he was thinking this is critical in that if you are a God like .Ra who wants to play God then one can manipulate this fact and make his thoughts hidden from the creator having said that then is it a coincidence that JFK was shot at this angle as well as if being witnessed from the Texas School Depository?

Now let's breakdown everything and illustrate the when situation and the how then the why looking at all this we can see that this is not a coincidence but clever calculates plan to deny JFK justice by making it impossible for him to present his case before .Ya [God] this is because if JFK is to be blasted at this angle then his brain thoughts in this Trajectory will dissipate automatically that alone means God not being able to receive his arguments in his defense but someone we can see that someone who is un unlikely source helped him present his case before .Ya

Now if we Ask why this is so then this is the answer at 33 degrees Trajectory a bullet will travel faster than the speed of light but as good as brain thoughts this is because of the law of uniqueness and the law of representations the law of uniqueness states that when a person tries to hide from something in trajectory the effect is for that thing to stop him thinking that means hide at the expense of your thoughts that also means who ever ducked did so at the expense of their thinking in such a way that hiding at that angle would stop and brain thinking to react to the situation that means at the very moment the bullet was fired all those who ducked simply stopped thinking as well hence no reaction that means if we are to ask after the effect no one among those who ducked would give you a sound answer because all those were not thinking at the time they ducked hence probably the need for two shooters the first one just a pasty to make everyone duck as he fire a shot then the second one to make all be ducked when the 33 angled bullet came by when all were ducked rendering them unable to think for that split second this can be true considering that the FBI were behind the Assassination of JFK through their man Elvis Lungton in Evolution of Democracy I said that he was [Elvis Langstan]

Now if we Ask what can be then this is the answer Edgar J Hoover then gay and being FBI chief resorted to targeted attacks of the Kennedys we can only assume that he targeted the Kennedys because of their fame but we must also give them credit as JFK was not as straight with anyone as he wanted everyone to believe after successive failures to ejaculated with his wife Jackie Kennedy due to inserted FBI agent number 7868388284206 that threatened either to break his dick or chew it or for it to freeze in a big-hole position the FBI had attached this to Jackie's vagina making JFK not feel a thing all this in order to push him to one they regarded as a half-wit Marylyn Monroe in the end after 3 straight months he succumbed to the pressure where he would have sex with her once only and then help her kill herself through administering himself a cocktail of pills that would eventually kill her Now this is what they might have had against the president if it was revenge for this then the FBI made sure that in death the president will not have a chance to stand before Go [.Ya] and present his creation case this they made it sure by carefully placing two assassins one above the other in exact symmetry so that both trajectories if combined together will ban JFK to even be allowed to present his case in the Afterlife before God, the Council of Creation, The Devil and .Ra one of the gods

that means everything was a predefined act that will result in the death of the president of the United States at the hands of the FBI who we now know to swear by the God. Ra

Now if we Ask why this is the answer .Ra is the chief Supreme of justice and order and as such would match the FBI rather than anyone else that means they have carefully studied .Ra and know most of the critical issues to address

Now if we look at predefined plan here is a glimpse of the plan

1 corner JFK to commit a crime and then use that to leverage an even more sinister case against him

2 illicit any help and fast using the victim as a child that needed protection and not murder

3 ask JFK to joke about life and to chose death instead [something done throughout the Texas dinner before his death] this means that surrendering his rights to face .Ya according to Yahweh's creation manuals if we look at this we can see that .Ya forbids Bargaining with the devil if you want heaven today we have discovered the creation manuals of the devil here it is

Devil's Creation Manuals

1 don't accept heaven but hell only

2 never mention acetate or ask it for help ever

3 never call acetate for help

4 never acetate here acetate there

5 all other creation manuals by the devil forbids anything to do with acetate up to creation manual number 200 that alone points to his fear of acetate

Now let's Ask a lot of questions at this point if we Ask what can be then this is the answer what is and what was could still be achieved If what was is the same as what if meaning we can restore JFK,'s soul into its body but the soul can not be revived until I used creation to raise

him up proof look into his picture deep and say whereareyou.start.now
Results I am in afterlife David Gomadza raised me up
Now back to the pre-planning we can see that the FBI predefined a lot of things so that the outcome could be easily achieved now let's recreate everything just to prove that this is what happened
1 JFK must not go to heaven but must be doomed to hell for eternity
2 JFK must not be given any chance to speak to Go [.Ya]
3 JFK must not be able to speak in order to present his case
4 even if he is to find a way to be in .Ya's presence he must not utter even a single word
5 what could be is that JFK must remain in hell with the devil
6 what would be is that forever he must be denied a chance to speak to Yahweh [God] a chance to speak before .Ya is forbidden because of his crimes against the people
7 if given a chance by .Ya then no words must come out of his mouth and .Yah must not hear a thing of what he is to think nor those brain thoughts
8 JFK must be locked in hell by the devil and be burned for eternity
9 must not plead before the council of creation, .Ra, .Ya or .devil
10 JFK must beg for mercy and not try to prove his innocents
11 JFK must surrender his soul to the devil
13 JFK must admit his guilty rather than plead with the gods for his innocents
Now let's look at how they did this
1 this was fixed by making sure that when he was struck his brain would dislodge the exit road for his soul so that his soul is stuck in his brain this is what happened on the day of his assassination the soul of his could not find the exit out of his body as the blasting by a bullet removed this passage that it was stuck this are the emotional brain commands at the time
Iamtrapped.start
Doesanyonehearme.start
Helphelphelpx28ifanyonehearingrespondnow.start
Instantly something responded in his head the answer
exitnowriskofdeath.start
At which he replied
iamJFKthepresidentriskofdeathbodyincapacitatedpassageremoved.start
Instantly something else awakes in his head and sends a message to .Ya
IamJFKpresidentoftheUnitedStatesofAmericaineedhelpiamstuckinhead.
start
Instantly something replied gotohell.start

Instantly he opened his eyes in hell where he protested iaminnocentthoesepeopletreatedmeasififwereagod.start instantly the .devil answered whyyoucomeherethen.start iamtrappedanddontknowhowtogotoheaven.start the devil looked lost for a while why then did you come to me .devil instantly JFK's heart started beating up fast scared .devil ihavenothingagainstyou.come soiamherebutishouldbepresentingmycase.Ya the devil asked the creation manuals to check why he ended up in hell if he didn't want hell 2 they blasted my head open and in so doing they removed the passage to the exit point that means I am trapped in here and have no way to go can .Ya help me come! Shouted the beautiful green-eyed Catitighit instantly JFK finds himself before the Council of Creation, .Ra, God

God astonished looked at him expecting him to speak but nothing came out of him or his mouth or his brain to .Ya's surprise [what seems to be the problem surely the predefined parameters help you choose but this is worse than I thought the man fought back the tears they send me before my time through a lie if you know their deception then .Ya you would let me present my case before you otherwise what is the value of life and creation I here challenge you .Ya using the first amendment right of creation that says everyone must be heard in a fair trial above all these people presented me as a God when I am human that alone is the reason why there is creation to come and defend ourselves before you Yahweh

Now that we qualified the circumstances in which he died let's look at the implications of what was done to him as I have pointed out before his injuries are not coincidental but a president just like a king to be martyred but only that if he is there it is no use because how could he present his case when he has no voice but its a different story with the gods in that the gods can easily read his brain thoughts and know what he is thinking that could explain his case but...

The workers of the god .Ra were at work in the likes of the FBI who knew a little bit more and were willing to deny him this chance but how the FBI through their man Elvis Lungston blasted JFK in the head to deny him and his soil exit rights above all blasted him in the throat so that he can speak and even if he did at 33 degrees angle .Ya will not decoded his thoughts a reminder that JFK was shot in the head and neck. This means that whoever was behind his assassination knew a little about this especially the bullet to the throat

Now let's Ask a lot of questions

1 could the shot to the throat meant to damage the voice chords

2 what could be the purpose of the short in relation to the execution then to the arguments about creation before Yahweh
3 what can be
4 what could be
5 what was to be could be
6 what is to be could be
7 What was to be
Now if we look at the charts below we can see that JFK was assassinated so that he can never be allowed to speak or defend himself if we look at the practice it dates back to the time of Charles 1 of England and if we Ask why then this is the answer divine kings believed in appointment by birth right they were chosen to be representatives of God on earth by direct appointment that is through God himself if we Ask what can be and what would be these are the answers the kings would be God's representatives on earth and martyrs of the people
Now what could be they could easily be killed by a mob because of this if we Ask what can be then this is the answer we can always ask what can be but how this is so now we must ask also several questions can we ask why JFK was blasted in the head especially where he was blasted considering that that is the place of the exit of his soul? Can we ask why this is so it is because JFK was charged with treason and as such had to be blasted also that treason means fighting the king a representative of God hence denial of access to plead with God and all this makes JFK be blasted
Now let's look at the codes in play I think you will appreciate the bran from here lanyards because here is the masterpiece
JFK jumps into the limousine and waves his hand at the people saying "I shall be your president" instantly a new message received rings in his temple lobby Mr. JFK we can here you louder and clear later he can hear a message being read converting nerve impulses and Action Potentials instantly as this is happening something jumps out of him and into the air this then goes to the couple who then into the room Then into one of them who then cried profusely but asked what can be done instantly he looked lost and asked what happened this time something ran out of him and into the person in front of him then into the other person then died a closer look at all this reveal that JFK on the day he died had been visited by ghost like figures that entered inside him just before he was blasted A closer inspection reveal that these were some kind of ghost binary numbers that carry people away just before death if this is true then JFK could gave been shot earlier than

this but how come If we Ask this is the answer can JFK have been shot earlier than this and why

The answer unlikely even though the binary reverse [,hell,] came way too early than expected now if we Ask more questions then this is the answer what would bring these way early apart from death itself when a person dies these always comes to move things around looking at JFK he might have triggered these by constantly denying heaven so this triggers the hell boys to come early

Now let's move on the day he was shot JFK had denied heaven 3 times as a joke during dinner after that he had asked someone to pray for him saying o lord just say o my lord this is a passage from the devils creation manual that might have seemed as paying allegiance to the devil so that he started cursing which in turn made those who were listening mad at one point we could here [check] this Elvis Lungstan cursing hard at JFK but without communication going on between them

Elvis Lungstan got off a bus [reading his brain scans] and rushed to the Texas School Depository he entered the building and went up to the top level the fourth floor there he literally bumped into Lee Harvey Oswald because he said [get out of my way punk] a closer reading reveal an Oswald Harvey being pushed by an agitated man out of the way. If these man knew each other then they would have spoken

Later somehow Lee Harvey Oswald took the exact same position with his own rifle but a lower level than Elvis Lungstan's position

The Analysis

Ceteris paribus if we add the Trajectory of bullets between Elvis Lungstan and Lee Harvey's the effect is to make the bullets have the same Trajectory but here is the catch for the bullet to cause the 33 Trajectory effect of making everyone stop thinking there must be a first bullet that sends people ducking so that when the 33 Trajectory bullet comes everyone will already be ducked meaning at it passes it creates the 33,8999910 depression that causes all brain thoughts to run into this depression and literally dissipates

This is the classic thriller people like the FBI would use if it's them killing the President because this ensures that when he was being shot no one's brain would be working to see what happened to record or witness anything the questions to ask are these were there any witnesses that came forward with exactly what happened or there were so many accounts that not even one was believable

If we Ask what else can prove this theory we can look at the Zapruder film

A closer inspection reveal Lee Harvey Oswald kneeling down in the Texas School Book Depository aiming at JFK as he aim to take him out he started cursing his own words from his brain

"Mr. President your fingerprints are all over my girlfriend she is pregnant if you can respect that then I have no choice but to blast ...a gunshot rocketed above the floor he was he looked confused [brain scans] if it's not me then there is someone up above that means I am the pasty the one to die but...I was supposed to be the lead [panicked] if I am the pasty then I die sense of fear quickly dropped the gun just before the second shot again rocketed the sky blasting JFK's head off instantly he looked out through the window and someone pointed at him he froze but got up and ran towards the stairs going upstairs where the shots came from instantly a man walked out and froze on his site he said to him Lungstan the lead your man is downstairs apac.org.out a quick search on the internet did not bring anything but closer look again makes sense that he might actually have said a.pac.org.out if this is so then during that time This was a code used by the FBI to ask someone to accompany him as his shield until he was safe
Now let's quickly recap because even better we have live dialogue between the soul of JFK and .Ya [God]
If we are all on this then this is exactly how this was planned
EL abbreviation for Elvis Lungstan was the lead to take out JFK clean and nice and walk away with flying colors Oswald was supposed to get frightened and not shoot at all in case someone finds him first but if he did not fire the bullet why would the Trajectory from his floor be used the answer he would help fuel conspiracy theory because the floor he was and the bullet Trajectory would not match raising suspicion of whether he really killed JFK but if he was the killer then the bullet Trajectory would not have had any effect on peoples thinking whatsoever hence no one would have suspected of anything regarding the magic angle 33 degrees
Now could have what if we are to ask a question What happened and why we know for sure Oswald wanted to shoot JFK he only did not because of Lungston who took the fatal shot and blasted JFK at point blank now if you want to know what can happen to JFK then ask what if this is the answer JFK was blasted by Elvis Lungstan who was the lead and the pasty was Oswald now this is something you never heard before Oswald and Lungstan knew each other in fact they were put on this mission on same day but separately this is proof Elvis's brain scan Oswald must just cover me until I out of the city

Oswald I must follow Lungstan out or I am the pasty
Now we can also reveal that they secretly recorded everything themselves without knowing it I can tell you exactly what happened that day from digital audio residue found in both their brains
I am going to blast JFK and fuck KST but only if he can't comply with requested documents and payment of 72000 American dollars owed to me by CBZ studios [Edgar J Hoover]
If I miss then pasty must cover for me [Lungstan]
If I die Marin must go back to Russia with my kids [Oswald]
If you go make sure to say what.if [Langton talking to JFK at the dinner]
These are what are called reference points because as you will see these will play a key role in pinpointing who was who
But let's go back to the issue at hand why did they try to profit JFK to present his case before .Ya?
JFK was unable to fulfill a promise he made years before where he said that one day I will stand before God and tell him how I worked hard to make your life's better day and night this day Langton had challenged him saying that JFK was just for the devil because all he did was wrong, he prostitutes, he gambled with other people's lives and urinated in church and surely all this is associated with the road to hell Now if this were true then JFK could have opted for the hell road but he was a devote Christian so how come
JFK believed he had demons or something pit in by FBI to act as if demons were inside him
Now we can easily see that JFK had no issue with religion before until he got Marylyn Monroe killed It was JFK who administered all those pills that killed her in actual fact he had used a pillow to smoother her but she had already died in a split second since this day things had never been the same again his brain scan reveal a few days he kept asking what justice is there if someone just die like that he had not been himself too
Now if we Ask what could be then he could have been killed by a terrorist that same day he smothered Marylyn Monroe
Now that we clarified some issues with JFK now let's look at how they were go to stop him presenting his case before .Ya
1 Obstruct exit point of his soul
advised2 remove the voice to speak to Yahweh
3 ask him to say whatthefuck instead of what if
4 to skip crucial steps like ask what if when trapped inside the body
5 ask to beg for mercy

6 asked to make errors that are critical meaning denied heaven
7 could simply have stayed inside nb there is no hurry when going to hell
8 could have replied with a hell no
JFK new the consequences of his actions
Now that we have looked at this now we Ask a lot of questions that need answers
What can happen in hell
What could it be in hell
Could JFK be able to request to seen .Ya
Can JFK present his case and be heard
Can JFK chose heaven when he is in hell instead
How would he go to heaven from hell
What can be
What could be
What would be
What is to be
What can be
What would be
What was
What is
What would be
What could be
What has been
What would be
What then
What the fuck
How come
What can be
What would be after
What might be after
What the hell
What has been
What could be
Now Ask yourself these questions and see why going to heaven from hell is tricky
1 who you tell who can send you to heaven
2 who can ask on your behalf
3 what can be said
What to as
When to ask

How to ask
What can go wrong and how
What has happened before and how
What is to be is to be
How come
Now that we looked at the critical questions we can proceed what was JFK like when he was alive in terms of communicating with the devil and God
What could be that he said that influenced things
What would be if someone is to help him and who is likely to help him and why
What are the circumstances surrounding his death
Do all souls go to hell as default then plead to be sent to heaven
What can be of hell and heaven
What would be of hell and heaven
What can be said about hell and heaven interchangeably
What can go wrong between the two
Can JFK mistaken hell for heaven
Are there clear cut situations where it Says hell and where it says heaven
What are the circumstances surrounding JFK's death and the need to go to heaven or hell
Can someone else decide where one goes hell or heaven
Can the earthly court decide about heavenly things
What if JFK decides to take a short at heaven after
What can be of all this
What could be of heaven
What was of hell
What is of hell that can't be of heaven
Can angels go to hell
Can evil go-to heaven
Who decides what is what of what
What is to be must be or what?
JFK cried for help when he discovered that he was trapped after tye gun shot wound removed that passage out of the brain
Now he has two choices to cry so that Yahweh come to the rescue or to curse so that the devil come to the rescue
If we Ask him what would be his answer woo can be done JFK this is the answer I am stuck inside my own body the brain passage has been removed
JFK had two choices ask .Ya or .devil
He went to ask the devil for help to be sent to Yahweh this is odd

because you would not expect him to ask the devil for any help but he did his words

I am stuck in my own body and can't escape please send me to .Ya so that I can present my case before .Ya I believe I am a nice person and can't go to hell for eternity after all its these people's fault they tried to treat me like I am some kind of a God but wo am just human that in itself is the reason why we are in this mess in the first place God hear my case I am a nice good person if I go to hell then there is no justice because all I did is refuse to be treated like a God at my own expense the reason I am here so if they are to win then where is justice then You must make it hard for them by allowing me to go to heaven because everything they did was to deny me my basic right to present my case before you almighty God I say this because

1 they damaged the brain passage so that the spirit is stuck inside once stuck inside then the next stage is to ask the devil to send their binary based movers to take me to hell against my will and all the rules of creation

Above all this they have removed my voice so that I can't speak to you or that you can't understand Mr.

More over they castrated my penis today in the mortuary so that I won't know the road to hell or heaven I say so because they are using it to make me angry by waving it in my face all the time is this right before the laws of creation Yahweh?

The devil listened and stopped what he was doing [holding dead humans with his hands] if I let you go how are you going to present your case the voice has been damaged and the penis is removed for Yahweh listen to the whole body not just the voice I know .devil but I must try for this is not far the people of America are making a huge mistake for leaving me dead and for the dungeons when I should be in heaven

Instantly the devil constructed a paradigm and attached it to me JFK this thing was long and had an aerial but could only work for 10 seconds before switching off

I looked scared what I God was not going to hear me or my voice or feel my penis vibrate in support of my arguments

I knew I had a huge task so I thanked the devil even though I had refused his help he said I always say what then and this is reference to his kingdom the hell I stood up and staggered front with this long rod hooked on me but only for it to fall to the ground I cried again and picked it up and instantly Yahweh stood in my face that instead of being afraid I found courage I said Yahweh God almighty how can the wicked prosperity and the thieves and muggers walk away when a president has to be stuck in the dungeons unfairly Lindon Johnson betrayed the Constitution by collaborating with the people to betray the president and get him killed if it wasn't for them I could still be alive Now hear my case I present before you I swear I never expected the head shot even though I felt it it caused so much commotion within my body I died and died and died and died and still now I am still dying do you know that Lindon Johnson was a physicist a doctor? What he did is get me stuck inside so that panic and fear kill me a second time if it wasn't forb the .devil then I could be here but without a voice or a head for that matter now I will tell you everything only because I am damaged and I am afraid that even though I was assures you know everything this case is different. Lindon Johnson removed my voice but look where the help is coming from? From an unlikely source from the .devil himself what are the chances?

The .devil created a system where my breathing is only for 10 seconds to sustain life only but cleverly something I have never heard that 10 seconds is all I need to send messages out of the head as brain thoughts That means that every 19bseconds I will tell you my arguments and present my case before you ask me what about the voice I will tell you in advance that the clever .devil has also devised a method where the frequency of the bullet acts as my voice based on 2 principles

1 the law of uniqueness that says some things if put at the same time will become one and the other that means that the frequency of the bullet is now my voice so that after 10 seconds the bullet noises you will hear will be the same as my human voice and we shall use this equation

Z= voice + frequency of bullet + consonant where everything is equal

That means that z is the value of my voice as the frequency of the bullet that means that is z is w then my voice is wwwww [5] where 1 is equal to 5 everytime

Now if the bullet frequency is s then my voice is sssss

Now let's work out an alphabetic order that will correspond to all bullet frequencies

a = a5

b = b5

c = c5

...

z = z5

Now if I say cg then the word is seemed but my consonants sre still there we must use reverse image mirroring so that if I say sssssggggg

that means gggggsssss
The reason being that when speaking action potentials comes first but when thinking action potentials comes second
Now I hereby present my case before you .Ya almighty God
Humans have become the pitfall of themselves seeking revenge when they should be giving forgiveness everyone is now obsessed with judgmental thoughts instead of understanding and peace
The American people gave collided with foreigners and have held their own president at ransom asking for his blood so that they say he is a traitor and must die I want you .Ya, .devil [pause looking at .devil shocked and felt like crying] .Ra and the Council of Creation to all you I present a new chapter in mankind I present a new world that is full of hope all my life I preached for hope and look how hope has drove the theme even here [paused and looked around to see where he was] hell but that has everyone in it namely that creature with [started counting heads] 9 or 8 heads that shine like a Christmas tree then to .Ra I know .Ra from Egyptian mythology and to you creature with [he paused and realized that something was wrong so he asked quickly] where is .Ya then, where is .devil I know .Ra and I guess everyone else is part of the Council of Creation
Never mind I am hereby to present my case in JF. Kennedy [smiles internally touching his head- place where if humans head would be instantly the creature lifted its wings and flapped the wings hard
I heard you correctly but I have predefined set of rules that are never at fault for a billion years
Oh Yahweh it's you, it's me Yahweh JF. Kennedy I know all this but you must understand that even though your predefined parameters work humans have tampered with the system the reason why we are here today do you think that if this was not true then why would we have gathered here today I want you .Ya to know that humans have become manipulative and devious to cheat and trick your predefined parameters if this is not true then you tell me how I could have got out if it wasn't for the .devil I might have been ejected to hell forever unfairly
The creature roared and said okay if you insist then you can go to heaven
JFK cried profusely and rejoiced saying this is a great day for humanity
Instantly a huge cry over heard all over the place saying humanity has changed the rules of creation saying leave space leave space instantly the couple started going in. A frenzy saying Yahweh! Yahweh!
JFK found the huge iron rod heavy to keep lifting

Yahweh can you restore my voice and head again my lord
Instantly something started flying around flapping its wings
Today Yahweh has restored fully a man who had already died
One of the angels said .Ya but xyzrstuvwxyz will not work after the person has died [translated as hearing ears and focal eyes that are at the back in the waste with a long focal beam that shines and one which the eyes follow around .Ya lifted his right hand and said
Behold I have restored everything on this man JFK for he shall live in heaven forever
JFK knelt down and prayed profusely but before he even finished one angel questioned why people who died and without the xyzrstuvwxyz should not find life hard in here
The lord God answered what the lord has repaired not any men asunder it
JFK cried
The end.

THE FUTURE

I decoded the brain and found the Almighty king Yahweh.
One day the world will realize that we have fulfilled creation.

Who is in the Council of Creation
.Ya
.devil
.Ra
Council of Creation

Creation according to the devil

1. Do everything wrong from day one until day you die
2. Hate everything good and love the devil and evil.
3. Don't listen to Acetate and never accept help from acetate ever forever.
4. – 500 talks about hating acetate.

Creation according to God
[already covered]

ABOUT DAVID GOMADZA

Visit www.twofuture.world

www.ingramcontent.com/pod-product-compliance
Lightning Source LLC
Chambersburg PA
CBHW051406250726
48656CB00006B/2304
* 9 7 9 8 3 2 3 9 0 6 5 0 5 *